Legends of Hollywood: The Life and Legacy of Marlene Dietrich

By Charles River Editors

Hans Georg Pfannmüller's 1954 caricature of Dietrich performing cabaret

About Charles River Editors

Charles River Editors was founded by Harvard and MIT alumni to provide superior editing and original writing services, with the expertise to create digital content for publishers across a vast range of subject matter. In addition to providing original digital content for third party publishers, Charles River Editors republishes civilization's greatest literary works, bringing them to a new generation via ebooks.

Introduction

Marlene Dietrich (1901-1992)

"Glamour is what I sell, it's my stock in trade." – Marlene Dietrich

When Marlene Dietrich first became a household name in the United States, she introduced a new standard for female sexuality on screen. Her performance in *The Blue Angel* (1930) not only stands as one of the most glamorous roles ever played but also one of the frankest depictions of the femme fatale ever captured on screen. Moreover, the film essentially set the tone for the image that Marlene Dietrich would cultivate over her career: unabashedly sexual but wrapped in an air of mystery. Most stars are beautiful and talented in ways that make them noticeable, but it is generally counterbalanced by an approachability that renders them accessible to a diverse audience. Marlene Dietrich, on the other hand, did not follow this model; ever since *The Blue Angel*, her star persona has rested on a foundation of exoticism.

Of course, the mythical qualities of Dietrich's image were no accident. Her most famous director, Josef von Sternberg, did his best to accentuate the foreign and exotic nature of his most famous actress, and in conjunction with that, the most famous images of Dietrich portray her glowing face juxtaposed against a shadowy silhouette, with the ornamental composition making it seem almost as though she were an artificial creation. Her life off-screen was no less exotic, as they were filled with an endless string of affairs that only enhanced the Marlene Dietrich myth.

At the same time, however, there is a complexity to her performances that extends far beyond the artificiality of the costumes and the sensuality of her appearance. The significance of Dietrich's career lies in the way that she combined feminine sensuality with masculine independence; she may have introduced a more overt form of female sexuality to cinema, but her films also inaugurated a female independence that had yet to surface in Hollywood. Moreover, the narrative of her life reveals much about both German and Hollywood, as well as the cabaret culture of Berlin and the politics of Nazi Germany and America before and after World War II. Film stars become famous for their performances, but they are not separate from the cultures in which they operate.

Legends of Hollywood: The Life and Legacy of Marlene Dietrich profiles the life and career of one of Hollywood's most iconic actresses. Along with pictures of important people, places, and events, you will learn about Marlene Dietrich like you never have before, in no time at all.

Chapter 1: A Prussian Upbringing

"I am at heart a gentleman." – Marlene Dietrich

Marie Magdalene Dietrich was born on December 27, 1901 in Schoneberg, which is now a subset of Berlin, but in turn of the century Germany it was still an autonomous unit that would not merge with Berlin until 1920. As with many other film stars, the name given to her at birth was not the same one with which she would be identified later in life. Marie Magdalene was a very common name in Germany at the time, and in an urge to separate herself from the others with her name, at age 11 she conflated her first and middle names to form "Marlene." She had one older sibling, Elisabeth, who was born one year before Marlene, and the two were the only children of Louis Erich Otto and Wilhelmina (Josephina) Elisabeth Dietrich. The family lived in a small flat in Sedenstrasse, a street named after a famous battle of the same name (Bach).

Dietrich's house in Schoneberg

Marlene's parents came from dissimilar backgrounds, although arriving at the true facts surrounding her childhood has always been a challenge. Over the years, there have been many false claims made about Marlene's family, with spurious allegations that were due in no small part to Dietrich's own habit of disclosing false information with regard to her upbringing. Dietrich was fond of misleading the public, a habit that only enhanced the mystery of her image, but regardless, it is now believed that Josephina came from a vastly more privileged background than her husband. Her family had amassed a generous endowment from their involvement in the clock making trade, and Marlene's mother was raised in an environment of moderate affluence. Josephine's family also embraced a strict Prussian culture built around a harsh sense of discipline; despite her family's socioeconomic status, she valued hard work and imparted this upon her daughter. Biographer Steven Bach explained, "Josephine, like the daughter she would bear, had a mind and will of her own and cared more about character and breeding than social position. One of her favorite words was *stable*, an allusion to pedigree, and she viewed it as the source from which all blessings flowed, from godliness to good teeth…Happiness might come, but diligence and duty were more to the Prussian point." (Bach 16).

Josephine's emphasis on diligence and hard work may seem antithetical to the glamorous lifestyle that Marlene cultivated as she became famous, but Bach's description of Marlene's mother reflects the immense amount of work that Marlene herself poured into her own profession. Throughout her life, Marlene expressed a kinship toward her mother, and while Josephine's domestic lifestyle bore little in common with Marlene's glamorous one, mother and daughter possessed a shared Prussian sense of discipline.

Conversely, Marlene's father did not come from a wealthy background, but he was upwardly mobile, rising through the ranks of German society by virtue of his military career. Prussian culture extolled the virtues of the military, and a great deal of importance was placed on a man's uniform. For years, a spurious rumor circulated that Louis had been a hero in the Franco-Prussian War of 1870-71, but this is clearly false, since he was born in 1868 and would have been far too young to fight in that war. Still, Louis did improve his social standing significantly after that crucial war by becoming a lieutenant in the police force. Bach notes:

> "Police Lieutenant Dietrich was…a good-looking man by fin de siècle standards, with the full chest and stout bearing that suggested strength of character. He was not tall or wasp-waisted in the dashing imperial fashion, but sturdy, with a handsome broad face and deep-set eyes a daughter would inherit one day, a straight nose, a Kaiser Wilhelm mustache winging above an oddly melancholy mouth, and an erect military bearing that kept his tunic taut and the spike of his *Pickelhaube* pointing upright and true." (Bach 13).

Marlene's father was a broad man, but while his build may have "suggested strength of character," his looks belied a lazy character at odds with that of his wife. During his career in the military, he acquired a reputation as a ladies' man, making it odd that he married a woman as disciplined as Josephine. Moreover, Josephine's rather plain appearance stood in stark contrast with her husband's dashing charm, and her virtue and wealth clashed with Louis's more humble background. Their marriage was clearly an example of opposites attracting, and the two married in 1898, with Marlene's sister born roughly two years thereafter.

At first, Marlene's parents were happily married, and the family lived in relative comfort. They even owned a telephone, a major status symbol of the time period, and they employed servants to assist in caring for the children (Skaerved). However, over time, Louis's ambition began to wane, and he revealed himself to be unsuitable for marriage. It has been argued that his motives in marrying Elisabeth were less than honorable, and that he was simply attracted to her substantial dowry, but whatever the reason, Louis was not a model father and maintained a less than consistent presence in the household. (Skaerved). Over time, his status within the police force slipped as well, shifting from Lieutenant to the lowest rank. It seems Louis was attracted to the social status of the police officer but ultimately unwilling to commit to the rigors and requirements of the job itself. As his rank slipped, the family was unwilling or unable to maintain their lifestyle, and they moved continuously during Marlene's early years. By the time she was 6, the family had already relocated four different times. In 1906, Louis and Josephine separated (but did not divorce), and moving forward Marlene was effectively raised by her mother and grandmother.

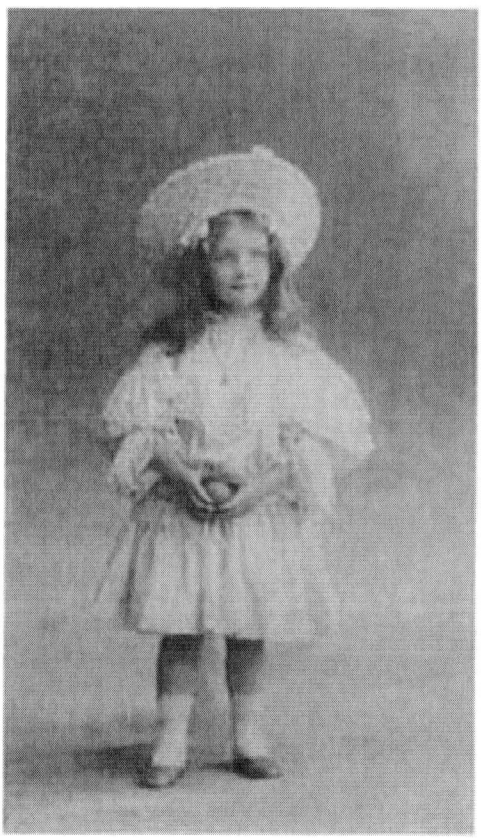

Marlene as a young girl

After separating from his wife, Louis continued to carry on affairs with a number of women, which eventually led to him contracting syphilis, which brought about his untimely death in 1907. For years, it was reported that Marlene's father had passed away due to a heart attack associated with a horseback riding accident, but this story was fabricated in an attempt to shield his ignoble cause of his death. Even though her relationship with Louis had long since turned acrimonious, Elisabeth mourned her husband's death deeply and would continue to wear only black throughout Marlene's childhood.

Despite the family difficulties, her father's death, and the somber mood of her mother, Marlene did not have an unhappy childhood. In fact, her autobiography referred to her time with her mother and grandmother in fond terms, and she speaks of her grandmother in an almost idolatrous fashion: "My wonderful and gentle grandmother…was not only the most beautiful of all women but also the most elegant, the most charming, and most perfect person that ever lived. Her hair was dark red and her eyes of an iridescent violet-blue. She was tall and slim, ever radiant and cheerful…My grandmother showered me with love, tenderness, and kindness…My grandmother was at one and the same time very real and very mysterious, a dream image, perfect, desirable, distant, and fascinating." Thus, while Louis's premature death was certainly a tragedy, the effects of his passing were mitigated by Marlene's close relationship with her mother and grandmother.

Marlene consistently stated that as a young child she was pale and thin, with reddish-blond hair that accentuated her whitish complexion (Dietrich). While this description would not suggest the appearance of a great beauty, Marlene also noted that from an early age strangers would compliment her on her appearance; when walking with her sister, they would specifically remark that Marlene possessed a beautiful face while neglecting to praise her sister's appearance. Liesel apparently inherited Josephine's facial features, while Marlene acquired her father's high cheekbones and general physical attractiveness, but there was no sibling rivalry between the two. The children simply accepted this, and it seems Liesel did not share the gregarious personality Marlene had inherited from Louis anyway.

The death of Marlene's father did not darken her childhood, but it inevitably produced significant changes in the family's lifestyle. Josephine possessed large sums of family money, but with her husband's death she was forced to provide for the family with a widow's pension. Until the age of 6, Marlene was tutored at home, but in 1907 the two sisters entered formal schooling for the first time when they were enrolled at the August-Viktoria school, an all-girls institution in Charlottenburg. Josephine's tutelage gave Marlene a strong grounding in academics, she was talented in music (particularly the lute, piano, and violin), and she knew not only German but also some French and English. From the beginning, Dietrich was always more committed to her musical studies than the classroom, while Liesel was more proficient in the traditionally academic courses.

In the wake of her father's death, Marlene experienced a docile upbringing, but with the arrival of World War I, the family relocated to Dessau, where Marlene entered the Antonetten Lyzeum. Despite the fact that Marlene was never fond of her studies, it was during her time there that she met her first romantic crush: her French teacher, Marguerite Breguand. Far from a passing attraction, decades later Dietrich would refer to Breguand in terms similar to those she used when describing her grandmother: "She banished my loneliness, my childish worries, my sadness. She embodied both my wishes and their fulfillment. I spent all my free time thinking up gifts for her." Unfortunately, Breguand died during the war, and shortly thereafter, Marlene's schooling was compromised as efforts were made to assist the war effort. Students placed their academic studies on hold and made supplies for soldiers, and domestic classes concentrated on cooking with the sparse supplies available, so children learned how to prepare basic meals using limited ingredients like potatoes, turnips, and other such items.

World War I had a pronounced effect on Marlene. Not only did it result in the loss of her beloved French teacher, but the conflict also instilled in her a sense of patriotism and appreciation for the efforts of soldiers. Later in life, she would be remarkably patriotic in expressing her gratitude toward the Allied soldiers during World War II. In addition to sparking Marlene's patriotism, Josephine married for a second time during World War I, this time to Eduard von Losch, a soldier whom she had known for several years. The circumstances for the marriage were unusual, because von Losch was wounded and he and Josephine were wedded over his hospital bed. In fact, he died just one week after they married, making clear that the rationale behind their decision was borne more out of practicality than any romantic love (Bach). In marrying von Losch, Josephine acquired his name and his death pension, but in return Josephine was tasked with caring for his mother, an obligation she accepted after his passing.

Thus, in the aftermath of his death, Josephine relocated once again, moving to an apartment in Kaiserallilee in Berlin. By this time, Marlene had just one year of schooling remaining, and she enrolled at the Viktoria-Luisen-Schule in April 1917 for her final year of study. As a teenager, Marlene had become increasingly conscious of her physical beauty, and in a development that (coincidentally) preceded the plot of *The Blue Angel*, Marlene became a sort of siren for her male professors. At the same time, she had difficulty applying herself toward her studies and quit school in 1918, shortly before she was due to graduate.

The end of the decade was a busy time for both Berlin and the Dietrich household. During the late winter of 1919, Marlene's grandmother passed away, resulting in a generous inheritance for Josephine. At the same time, postwar inflation robbed her of her money, and Josephine suffered greatly. The climate of Berlin also changed, with the unstable social landscape of postwar Berlin resulting in the flowering of cabaret culture and a devil-may-care attitude that consumed the population. Coming to believe that Berlin was no place for Marlene to come of age as an adult, Josephine arranged for her daughter to head to Weimar, where she was to continue her music studies.

Marlene arrived in the Weimar region in October of 1919 and moved into a boarding house that saw her share a bedroom with five other girls. In Josephine's view, the environment would provide Marlene with the discipline and high-level instruction needed to advance as a musician. At the same time, however, Marlene's move to the Weimar region should not be interpreted as a forceful imposition on the part of her mother. Marlene was truly passionate about her musical practice and endeavored to become a musician.

In light of her later success as a solo performer, it is easy to lose sight of the fact that Marlene's talents as a singer developed well after her attempted career as a violinist. She dedicated herself to her studies, achieving a high level of proficiency that she had never reached in the classroom. Furthermore, just as she had been unafraid to play the role of temptress in her formal studies, she was not afraid to perform a similar role with her violin teacher, Professor Reitz. Marlene was notorious for showing up for her lessons in clothing that was transparent or otherwise revealed much of her physique, and it's now believed that she and Reitz engaged in a longstanding affair during her time in the Weimar. But regardless of his attraction to his student, Professor Reitz was unable to procure any professional breakthroughs for Dietrich, and her career as a concert violinist swiftly came to an end before it ever truly began thanks to a wrist injury she suffered in 1921. With little reason to remain, she moved back to Berlin that same year.

Chapter 2: The Roaring Twenties

"If [Marlene] had nothing more than her voice, she could break your heart with it." – Ernest Hemingway

Whether or not Marlene Dietrich actually possessed the talent to succeed as a violinist is impossible to adequately determine. At the time of her injury, she was still in need of significant practice, but the discipline she acquired from her mother may have led to professional success. As a result, the wrist injury unquestionably played an instrumental role in the chain of events that led to Marlene's eventual decision to pursue singing and stage performing, which in turn led to her film career.

In any event, at a time in which Dietrich was learning how to perform, the raucous environment of postwar Berlin was the ideal match for her. She engaged in affairs not only with men but also with women, including a close friendship with Gerda Huba, an aspiring writer who also worked as a librarian. On the one hand, inflation devastated the Berlin economy, but the care-free nature of the citizenry gave rise to a cabaret culture and a more open attitude that seemed to offer limitless opportunities for musical performance and sexual experimentation. Biographer David Ryan noted:

> "To dally in the Berlin of the 1920s was to see life in all its infinite variety. Men who felt unmanned by the war dressed as women, women lacking strong shoulders to lean on were forced back upon themselves to search for the hard

masculine drive towards fulfillment or found it in strong women, still others were in an indeterminate no man's land between the two sexes. All was mixed and confused. Any new philosophy was seized upon and lived out to the full...The only demand was to follow your own star, and take it where it might lead." (Ryan 3-4).

Another aspect of German culture that grew in significance following the war was cinema. Germany had long possessed a rich film culture, and after World War I the main film studio in Germany, the Universum Film AG (UFA), was among the most powerful in the world, while talented directors like Fritz Lang, F.W. Murnau, and G.W. Pabst were coming into their own. Forever a democratic medium, film remained popular even during times of economic despair in early 1920s Germany, and as the economy improved even more people flocked to the cinema. Considering the prevalence of cinema in German culture, it should come as no surprise that Dietrich's first job after arriving in Berlin was as a violinist in a pit band that provided musical accompaniment for silent films. In an early example of Dietrich's sexuality impacting her career, she was fired after just four weeks, as the all-male band was distracted by her long legs. Well aware of what people thought of her legs, Dietrich would later muse "the legs aren't so beautiful, I just know what to do with them."

After losing her job in the band, Marlene progressed to the cabaret stage, where her overt sexuality was a boon rather than grounds for dismissal. Furthermore, she took voice lessons and was hired as a chorus girl with the Guido Thielscher's Girl-Kabarett, as well as with the Rudolf Nelson musical revues (Bach). Working with the orchestra may have brought her in close proximity to films, but working in the cabaret offered far greater preparation for her film career, as many of her films, including those she made with von Sternberg, borrowed heavily from the cabaret stage. A sort of German equivalent to the American speakeasy, the cabaret was a space in which individuals were freed of preexisting social expectations. Not only was sexual experimentation openly accepted, but female independence was expected. Film director and cabaret artist Volker Kuehn later asserted that Marlene was the perfect representative of the 1920s Berlin female:

> "Marlene was a real child of these 'roaring '20s'...Marlene was an independent person who was so emancipated that she didn't care a fig about what people thought of her. She lived whatever she wanted to, and that was at a time when she was not yet the big star, when it was not so easy to live that way...That was the wonderful thing about this type of woman. They didn't want to be the little homemaker at the stove. They didn't want to just mix in, they wanted to set the accents. Marlene did just that." (Riva and Stern 3).

Kuehn's description of Marlene as a poster child for 1920s Berlin is apt, and Marlene would never have been able to achieve success in cinema without the carefree sexual spirit she displayed in the cabaret. Still, for all of her love for cabaret culture, Dietrich's initial attempts at entering dramatic acting were unsuccessful. In 1922, she auditioned for Max Reinhardt's famous drama academy, which effectively served as a training ground for the four theatres he owned and operated, but she was denied admission (Ryan). Overcome with nerves, she delivered an awkward performance that relegated her back to the cabaret. Considering the confidence she later exuded on screen, it is surprising that she would suffer from anxiety in her audition, but Dietrich had no formal training as an actress. In fact, it's fair to wonder whether she would have gained admission even if she had not gotten stage fright.

One of the ironies of Marlene Dietrich's career is that despite being rejected by Max Reinhardt's theater school, shortly after her failed audition she was employed as a chorus girl in his theatres. Similar to her failed job as a violinist for silent films, being turned down by Reinhardt's school was ultimately fortuitous, because she first began gaining small film parts during her time employed as a chorus girl. Dietrich's first film was *The Little Napoleon*, which was produced by the European Film Alliance, an alternative to UFA that was established by Paramount in an attempt to capitalize on the German film market. The emergence of the European Film Alliance was indicative of the fact the German market remained almost entirely free of Hollywood's influence until the middle of the decade. However, the European Film Alliance met with an abrupt end, which delayed the release of the film.

As its name might suggest, *The Little Napoleon* was a historical biopic chronicling the life of Jerome Bonaparte, the little brother of Napoleon. Dietrich was relegated to a minor role, playing a maid, but despite the insignificance of the film and her role, she would not have difficulty finding employment in the German film industry over the remainder of the decade. After *The Little Napoleon*, Marlene appeared in two additional films during 1923. One of these, *Love Tragedy*, proved significant because she met her future husband, the actor Rudolf Sieber, on the set. They were married in May of that same year, and Marlene gave birth to a daughter (the only child she would ever have), Maria Elisabeth Sieber, on December 13, 1924.

Dietrich and Sieber

Neither her marriage nor her child derailed her professional ambitions. Dietrich continued to work on both the cabaret stage and the screen during the 1920s, but she did have great difficulty getting hired for any starring roles. She appeared in two films in 1926 and four in 1927, but it was not until the end of the decade that she began getting cast in starring roles. By 1929, she was a significant actress in UFA ranks, but she was never given the opportunity to work with acclaimed directors such as Lang, Pabst, or Murnau. It was not until later in 1929, when she was cast by Josef von Sternberg to headline *The Blue Angel*, that she received her first major breakthrough.

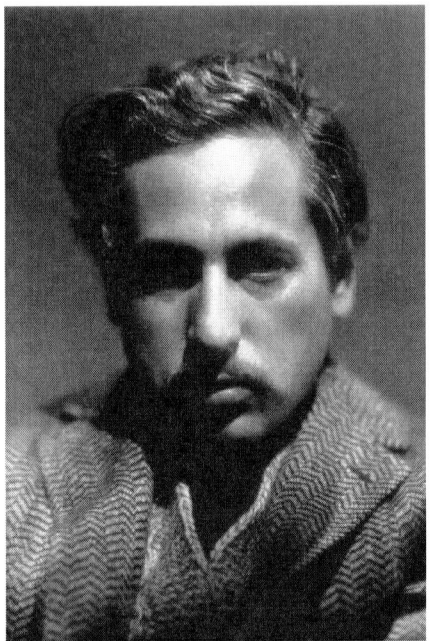

Josef von Sternberg

Chapter 3: *The Blue Angel* and the Move to Hollywood

"a serpentine lasso whereby her voice casually winds itself around our most vulnerable fantasies." - critic Kenneth Tynan's description of Marlene Dietrich's manner.

The Blue Angel remains the film with which Marlene Dietrich is most commonly identified, and this is with good reason, because her character is autobiographical in many respects. The film's plot features Dietrich starring as Lola-Lola, a performer at a cabaret club titled "The Blue Angel." Her performances draw the attention of the local schoolboys who are berated by their professor after they are so captivated by her performances that they are unable to concentrate on their studies. With the intention of berating his students at the cabaret, the professor visits the club himself and subsequently finds himself hopelessly enamored with Lola-Lola. He and Lola-Lola marry, and after losing his professorial position, she spends his savings. With no alternative, he accepts a position as a clown in the cabaret, only to watch as Lola-Lola becomes involved with other men. The professor ends the film stripped of all status, with neither his lover nor his profession.

Dietrich in *The Blue Angel*

It's not difficult to understand why Dietrich shot to fame in such a role, given that she spent much of the 1920s as a cabaret star and was thus an ideal fit for the role. Moreover, during her studies, she had cultivated a reputation for flirting with professors and even engaged in an affair with her violin instructor. In many ways, Dietrich was born to play the role of Lola-Lola. That said, she was still fortunate to even receive the role. The film was a major production, and even though Dietrich had recently risen to fame, she had not necessarily proven that she was capable of such a major film.

At her audition, Dietrich was evaluated by producer Erich Pommer, director Josef von Sternberg, and co-star Emil Jannings, and only von Sternberg was interested in giving the role to Dietrich. As producer, Pommer had yet to see that Dietrich would prove a worthy investment, while Jannings was understandably concerned that she would steal the spotlight from him. Jannings was one of the most recognizable film actors in Germany, and *The Blue Angel* was set to be his first sound film; in fact, as the film's chief star, he was largely responsible for enlisting the services of von Sternberg as director. Nevertheless, when it came time to cast the lead actress, von Sternberg's pick stood, thrusting Dietrich into the most prominent role of her young career.

Today, of course, those who watch *The Blue Angel* are left with no doubt that Marlene Dietrich fit the role like a glove, and that she was the appropriate choice for the role. By 1930, she had also progressed as a singer and gave memorable performances of the cabaret songs, including "Falling in Love Again" and "They Call Me Naughty Lola." Additionally, von Sternberg's formal style enhanced Dietrich's natural beauty. His camera lingers over her, and regardless of their status within UFA, there is no doubt that Dietrich is the star of the film. Before *The Blue Angel*, Dietrich had never worked with a director who rivaled the talents of von Sternberg, and he took her natural attractiveness and transformed her into one of the most exotic screen goddesses of film history. Through techniques such as high-key lighting, von Sternberg crafted shadowy compositions that created a glamorous and mysterious effect. The film eschews any attempt to present Marlene as a natural, matronly woman; she is brazenly glamorous and all the more arresting because of it.

    Because of von Sternberg's bravura directorial technique, it's tempting for some to consider Dietrich little more than a prop in his aesthetic design. James Naremore addresses this issue when he notes in reference to Dietrich, "Neither a realist nor a comic, she inhabits a realm where visible artifice becomes the sign of authenticity. She also challenges our ability to judge her acting skill, because her image is unusually dependent on a controlled, artful *mise-en-scene*" (131). This description identifies the way in which Dietrich's performance was indelibly associated with von Sternberg's work behind the camera, and the fact that her earlier films were not particularly successful further bolsters the notion von Sternberg was critical in developing her career. However, it would be an exaggeration to relegate Dietrich to nothing more than a decorative prop, because there is a complexity to her role distinct from the role she played in von Sternberg's ornamental compositions, as indicated by the fact that the gender politics of the Lola-Lola character have been subject to contrasting interpretations. On the one hand, some scholars, most notably Laura Mulvey (referring to Dietrich's performances in all of the von Sternberg films and not solely *The Blue Angel*) argues that Dietrich simply exists to satisfy the fetishistic gaze of the heterosexual male viewer. According to this view, the striptease attire donned by Dietrich allows viewers to inhabit a position of comfortable fetishism, positioning her character as one ultimately controlled by the gaze of the heterosexual male. On the other hand, critics such as Susan Sontag contend that Dietrich's character possesses a great deal of agency and is in fact a model for the independent female. Analyzing the Dietrich-von Sternberg collaborations, Sontag points to Dietrich's propensity to don male attire and the depth of her voice as motifs that suggest a countercultural resistance to male authority. In an age in which film roles for women were demeaning and (at best) patronizing, Marlene Dietrich's character offered a different model for women in film that gave them greater autonomy and was almost feminist.

    Both interpretations are defensible, but Mulvey's argument perhaps overvalues the way Dietrich is filmed while disregarding the effect she has on the viewer and her co-star within the narrative itself. Dietrich's glamorous figure certainly rewards the heterosexual male viewer, but viewers cannot overlook the fact that she is very much the aggressor and the narrative centers on her sending her male co-star into submission. In the end, much of the allure of the Dietrich persona lies in her ability to appeal to both male and female viewers, a motif noted by Rebecca Bell-Metereau when she wrote, "Dietrich's allure lies in her ability to appeal simultaneously to male and female audiences, an important factor in the viewer's appreciation of film…It is pleasurably disconcerting for either sex to identify with Dietrich, for the experience calls on both sexes to experience a liberating sexual duality." (104). Thus, watching Dietrich on screen elicits excitement in both men and women, but regardless of the gender of the viewer, her possession of male (voice) and female (body) characteristics engenders a complex response that forces the viewer to acknowledge the gender duality at work. As critic Kenneth Tynan put it, "She has sex but no positive gender. Her masculinity appeals to women and her sexuality to men."

Dietrich in 1933

Marlene Dietrich's performance is arresting because of her unusual appearance and the complexity of her character, but for all of her exoticism, it is also the case that *The Blue Angel* borrowed typical themes from the German cinema of the 1920s. This meant that *The Blue Angel* was really more exotic for an American audience than a German one. As noted earlier, UFA was remarkably successful (especially before 1925), and the German Expressionism genre was its defining category. Through films such as *The Cabinet of Dr. Caligari* (1920) and *The Last Laugh* (1924), viewers can see how the German Expressionism films emphasized the psychology of the characters, often to the detriment of the male lead. The femme fatale began to surface in films such as *Metropolis* (1927) and *Pandora's Box* (1929), and in this respect the German Expressionism films were early predecessors of Hollywood's noir films in the 1940s and early 1950s.

Following the completion of *The Blue Angel*, von Sternberg moved to Hollywood, where he was just the latest in a long string of German directors who would make the move overseas. Early in the decade, Ernst Lubitsch left for Hollywood, while F.W. Murnau moved overseas and was immensely successful with *Sunrise* (1927). Lubitsch signed with Paramount, the studio that was generally seen as the most highbrow and European, so it was only natural that Paramount would recruit von Sternberg, who at the time of *The Blue Angel* was easily one of Germany's most significant directors. Given that von Sternberg was Jewish, it was also advantageous for him to escape Germany, which by 1930 was already displaying the influence of the rise of National Socialism. But von Sternberg also realized it would be difficult for him to thrive in Hollywood without his major star, so he lobbied for Dietrich to move to Hollywood as well. Thus, in 1930 Marlene followed her director and joined von Sternberg in Hollywood, also agreeing to a contract with Paramount. She was given star treatment from the beginning, with a robust contract that paid her $1000 per week and a lavish apartment to live in.

The rather meteoric rise of Marlene Dietrich in 1929-1930 has historically been attributed to the guidance of von Sternberg, and Marlene herself acknowledged that he was able to accentuate her beauty more skillfully than the other directors with whom she worked (Dietrich). Over the years, von Sternberg was quick to claim credit for having discovered Dietrich, and there is an element of truth to his statement; by 1930, Marlene had acted in films for six years and never appeared in a truly monumental film. That von Sternberg lobbied for her to win the role of Lola-Lola against the judgment of the producer and leading actor also support the notion that von Sternberg rescued the actress from oblivion.

However, this also overlooks the fact that von Sternberg's reliance on his star actress was quite similar to Dietrich's dependence on the director. In fact, von Sternberg did not even direct another film during the time between *The Blue Angel* and his second collaboration with Dietrich. It is also true that von Sternberg himself never directed an exceptionally famous film before *The Blue Angel*, so it could also be argued that Dietrich made von Sternberg as well. Regardless, in order to continue directing internationally decorated films, von Sternberg relied heavily on Dietrich, and the two would complete six films together in Hollywood.

[margin note: each was instrumental in joint meteoric rise.]

Apart from appeasing their newly acquired director, Paramount also had clear motives for signing Dietrich to a contract. First of all, the international success of *The Blue Angel* strongly suggested that Dietrich's German exoticism could find great success with an American audience. Second, there was the risk of another studio signing the newly famous star. Finally, by the 1930s Paramount no longer had a monopoly on European émigrés. Earlier in the decade, Greta Garbo had signed with MGM, and the Swedish beauty was immediately successful with Americans. In addition, F.W. Murnau had moved to Hollywood just a few years earlier and had great success with *Sunrise*, produced by Fox. Thus, with Dietrich and von Sternberg under contract, Paramount had a clear response to Greta Garbo, and the subsequent films of von Sternberg and Dietrich would rival any of Murnau's efforts.

Greta Garbo

The Dietrich-von Sternberg films that succeeded *The Blue Angel* are noticeably different from their first film together. Not only was *The Blue Angel* the only film of theirs that was filmed in German, but the production values were more lavish on their Hollywood films, and Dietrich's acting style grew progressively more refined. For all the sensuality of her performance in *The Blue Angel*, von Sternberg saw room to build her glamour even further, and Dietrich went to great lengths to further enhance her image. Even though she had been far from overweight, she lost weight, the effects of which were most noticeable in her face, as the absence of any fat accentuated her cheekbones. Dietrich's friend, Erich Maria Remarque, described her appearance in his novel *Arch of Triumph*: "The cool, bright face that didn't ask for anything, that simply existed, waiting -- it was an empty face, he thought; a face that could change with any wind of expression. One could dream into it anything. It was like a beautiful empty house waiting for carpets and pictures. It had all possibilities -- it could become a palace or a brothel."

The two began their second film together almost immediately after Dietrich's arrival in the United States, and the film, *Morocco* (1930), was released in late fall of 1930. If *The Blue Angel* was over-the-top in its glamorization of Marlene Dietrich, *Morocco* and the later films in the von Sternberg-Dietrich cycle were even more extreme. In some respects, *Morocco* is very similar to the earlier film, most noticeably the fact that she plays a nightclub singer in both (although the German cabarets of *The Blue Angel* are replaced by a nightclub in *Morocco*). The basic plot involves Dietrich caught between two relationships, one with Legionnaire Private Tom Brown (played by Gary Cooper), and the other with a wealthy Frenchman named La Bessiere (Adolph Menjou.) In the end, Dietrich forgoes the opportunity for a life of wealth and chooses Brown, despite the knowledge that he is likely to die in the near future.

Morocco differs from *The Blue Angel* in that Dietrich's character is not as sadistic or self-serving; had Lola-Lola been faced with the predicament of choosing between a wealthy Frenchman and a soldier, she would almost certainly opt for the life of comfort. But for all the differences in Dietrich's character between the two films, the most notable difference relates to the costuming and formal elements. As one of the earliest sound films made in Germany, *The Blue Angel* appears almost raw in its sound synchronization, while *Morocco* has substantially more polish. In addition, there is a noticeable difference in Marlene's singing between the two films, and in *Morocco* viewers can for the first time recognize the vocal talents that led to her later success as a solo artist.

Of course, the most striking aspect of the film is von Sternberg's ornate costuming and mise-en-scene, which are flagrantly artificial in their campiness. One of the most challenging aspects of the film is the contrast between the film's plot - which is deeply dramatic on the surface with its look at the effects of war on interpersonal relationships - and the campiness of von Sternberg's technique. For this reason, James Naremore argues (in a discussion of the von Sternberg-Dietrich films as a whole), "In fact, the Sternberg films with Dietrich were a baffling mixture of commercial melodrama and extreme aestheticism, of dime-novel clichés and irony; even at their most self-consciously artistic, they were poised in a zone somewhere between romantic idealism, camp, and modernism, as if a certain tendency of Hollywood and late-nineteenth-century art had been pushed to such extremes that it began to deconstruct." (132-133).

Naremore's description identifies how the artificiality of the design threatens to undermine the plot to the point that the films become campy, but in spite of (or because of) this, viewers should not disregard the plots entirely. Like *The Blue Angel*, Dietrich's second film with von Sternberg contains a good deal of subversive material, especially as the masculine aspects of the Dietrich image that surfaced in *The Blue Angel* become even more pronounced in *Morocco*. In one scene, she performs a number in full masculine attire, including a top hat, black bowtie, and tailcoat, that has since come to be symbolically associated with Dietrich's star image. In another socially subversive scene, she kisses a woman. Both of these tested the limits of what was acceptable to an American audience in the early 1930s, cementing Marlene's exceptionally exotic status but also her place as a sort of provocateur in Hollywood.

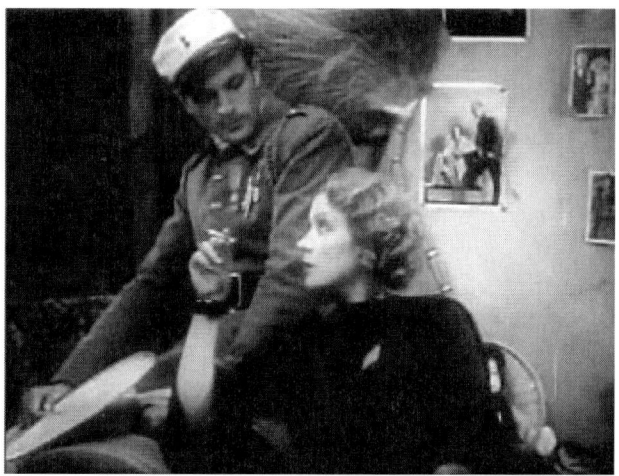

Marlene Dietrich and Gary Cooper in *Morocco*

That Paramount would permit Dietrich to kiss a female is surprising, but there's no question that if the film had been made five years later, such a scene would have been censored. *Morocco* was made immediately before the establishment of the Hays Code, and the film was made at a time in which Hollywood was growing more and more explicit and risqué in its treatment of sexuality. The emergence of the Busby Berkeley musicals, as well as the rise of the gangster genre, all signaled a tendency in Hollywood to test the limits of what was suitable to show on screen. Even though the Hays Code was technically established in 1930, it would not be regularly applied until a few years later, and *Morocco* is just one example of what made the early '30s the most sexually explicit period in Hollywood until the 1960s. Ultimately, the film was very well-received and was nominated for four Academy Awards, with Dietrich nominated for Best Actress and von Sternberg nominated for Best Director. Nominations for Best Cinematography and Art Direction further reflected von Sternberg's aesthetic talents.

The sexual provocation of Dietrich's character on the movie set was equally rivaled by the image she cultivated off-screen. Even though Marlene was technically still married to Rudolf Sieber, they had ceased living together by the time she moved to Hollywood, and though she did not hide her marital status, Dietrich engaged in a seemingly limitless string of affairs as soon as she reached America, later stating, "I've always been attracted to intelligent men. I can pick 'em in a full room, just like that. I don't care what age they are." Attempting to sort truth from rumor is exceptionally difficult because Dietrich was protective of her image, and later in life she was also notorious for giving conflicting accounts of her romantic activity, but according to her most reliable biographer, Steven Bach, Dietrich engaged in an affair with Gary Cooper, her co-star in *Morocco*. The fact they had an affair is surprising in light of Cooper's clean-cut image, and it's also believed that Cooper was jealous of the attention Marlene received from von Sternberg during the shooting of the film (Bach). Later in the decade, she carried on relationships (often concurrently) with actors Maurice Chevalier and John Gilbert.

In addition to her heterosexual affairs, it is now well-known that Dietrich was bisexual and had at least one high-profile lesbian relationship during the 1930s. Her close friend and confidant Mercedes de Acosta, a diminutive Mexican woman, was a love interest of hers (Bach). The Dietrich-de Acosta relationship is of particular interest since de Acosta had been a longtime lover of Greta Garbo, another female actress who was forced to keep her attraction to women a secret. Although the public was not aware of Dietrich's bisexuality or Garbo's lesbianism, stealing Garbo's lover only heightened the rivalry between the two famous actresses. Referring to famous European film stars of the 1920s and 1930s, Alice Kuzniar notes, "The most idolized actors and actresses of the period were to become gay and lesbian icons for years to come, Greta Garbo and Marlene Dietrich being the most famous" (30). It would not be until the mid-1950s, when Dietrich's film career had long been on the decline, that her lesbian affairs were unearthed.

Mercedes de Acosta

By virtue of the success of *The Blue Angel*, Marlene Dietrich was treated as a major star upon her arrival in Hollywood. Accordingly, this absolved her from the overbearing workload most actors and actresses were tasked with during their early years in Hollywood. In 1931, Marlene appeared in just one film, and she only acted in two in 1932 and one in 1933. Her acting career continued to be tied to von Sternberg to the extent that it was not until 1933 that she starred in a film made by a different director. In fact, Dietrich was in just one non-Sternberg film until their professional partnership ended in 1936.

If the list of films Marlene appeared in is not particularly robust, the demands placed on her in each film certainly compensated for it. It is well-known that von Sternberg was a brutally demanding director, and Dietrich was forced to submit herself to his authority on the movie set. In many instances, more takes than necessary were used to film a scene, with von Sternberg exercising an almost sadistic control over his actors. Even though the running times were well within the norms for the period, the films took a great deal of time to complete. The authority exercised by von Sternberg created a dynamic in which he was not unlike a svengali, and Dietrich was quick to acknowledge that working with him necessitated forfeiting control over her own image, explaining, "After Mr. von Sternberg took charge of my looks, sometimes I thought they belonged more to him than to me. The emphasis on the way I looked became a burden to bear, almost too great to enjoy." (Chandler 4).

 The anxieties expressed in her quotation are shared by many film stars, and it is no doubt difficult when one's physical appearance must be tightly monitored to adhere to the specifications of a director or film studio. Still, the Dietrich-von Sternberg relationship was different in that Marlene was portrayed in an extremely dissimilar way from any other actress. As her director, von Sternberg relied upon Marlene showing no signs of aging and retaining her icy façade, and in an age in which facial surgeries had yet to be developed, Marlene pulled back the skin on her face, holding it in place by using surgical tape cleverly concealed on screen. Every aspect of her face was without flaw. Her head was perfectly symmetrical, her eyes were regal in their haute expression, and her skin concealed any signs of wear. In order to appease von Sternberg, it was crucial that Marlene maintain this demanding beauty standard.

 Marlene's next film after *Morocco* was *Dishonored* (1931), an oft-forgotten film that cast her as a secret agent. More famous was Dietrich's film after that, *Shanghai Express* (1932), which was set against the backdrop of the Chinese Civil War. As the film's title suggests, the plot takes place on the train of the same name, and Dietrich plays Shanghai Lily, a courtesan who was once romantically involved with a doctor and British captain in the war. Predictably, the plot progresses toward their eventual reconciliation. The Chinese setting was in some respects a major departure from the films that first made Marlene famous, but playing a courtesan was not certainly not. The major difference separating *Shanghai Express* (and *Morocco*) from *The Blue Angel* is that in the Hollywood films her character eventually commits to her relationship with the male co-star. In this regard, the shift from Germany to Hollywood reflected at least a bit of the domestication of her image.

Marlene Dietrich in *Shanghai Express*

The domestication of Marlene Dietrich is at the heart of *Blonde Venus* (1932), the fourth film she made with von Sternberg. She stars as a housewife whose husband (Cary Grant) falls ill and does not possess the funds for his operation. In order to accrue the necessary funds, she accepts a job as a nightclub performer, which places her in contact with a wealthy audience member who she engages in an affair with. The film thus balances the two lives of Marlene the nightclub performer and Marlene the housewife. Eventually, she is welcomed back by her husband, another example of Dietrich ultimately submitting to a life of domesticity. Even as the film ends with a tidy resolution, however, the ending is essentially an afterthought, because the most memorable scenes in the film do not involve Marlene with her husband but rather her performances. In fact, von Sternberg was never campier than in *Blonde Venus*. In one scene, Dietrich performs her song in a gorilla costume before removing her costume in a chaste (although pre-Hays Code) form of striptease. With only three musical numbers performed, *Blond Venus* does not quite qualify as a musical per se, but like musicals, the song sequences are the most compelling parts of the film.

Dietrich in *Blonde Venus*

In 1934 and 1935, Dietrich starred in her final two films with von Sternberg. The first was *The Scarlett Empress*, which featured her as Catherine the Great. The film took extreme historical liberties, depicting Catherine as sexually promiscuous and even sadistic, but making a historical epic was an ideal premise for von Sternberg to showcase his baroque style. The palace is designed in an impossibly gaudy style, and Catherine's costumes are glamorously campy. *The Scarlett Empress* also offers some of the best examples of the shadowy butterfly lighting with which von Sternberg loved to depict Dietrich. By using shadows under the nose and chin, von Sternberg created a shadow that resembled a butterfly. The end result made Marlene appear glowing and bathed in an adoring light.

Dietrich as Catherine the Great in *The Scarlett Empress*

Analyzing the significance of *The Scarlett Empress* also requires considering the context of the 1930s, specifically the rivalry between Dietrich and Garbo. That same year, Garbo starred in *Queen Christina* (1933) for MGM, in which she also played Catherine the Great. While Garbo's role is reclusive, Marlene's is far more sexually explicit, and the two films demonstrate the central differences between their star personas. Both actresses were extraordinarily glamorous, but Marlene's allure was more self-consciously exotic than Garbo's more natural Swedish image.

The last of the films Marlene made with von Sternberg was *The Devil is a Woman*, which centers on the captivating effect Marlene's beauty had on men. The production was impacted by von Sternberg's notorious habit of issuing countless retakes, and the original male star, Joel McCrea, quit after being unable to deal with von Sternberg's directing. *The Devil is a Woman* was notoriously unsuccessful, and it became clear that while von Sternberg's style certainly succeeded in portraying Dietrich in a glamorous light, he was no longer able to attract the box office audiences necessary to subsidize such films. Consequently, the partnership between the famous director and star had come to an end.

The relationship between Marlene Dietrich and Josef von Sternberg forms one of the most complex aspects of the narrative of Dietrich's life. In all of her films with him, she played strong, independent women, but on the set she submitted to the harsh authority of the scrupulous director. If nothing else, the rapport between the two was passionate; it is well-known that Marlene and von Sternberg engaged in an affair, and viewers watching their films can certainly discern the passion von Sternberg held for Marlene. That said, they would never marry, nor would they work together after 1936.

Chapter 4: After Josef von Sternberg

"Glamour is assurance. It is a kind of knowing that you are all right in every way, mentally and physically and in appearance, and that, whatever the occasion or the situation, you are equal to it." – Marlene Dietrich

Considering that the films Marlene made with von Sternberg are by far the most famous of her career, it is perhaps surprising to note that they were all completed within a period of six years. By the time they separated in 1936, Dietrich was still just 35 years old, young enough to remain a major star in Hollywood. She was still under contract with Paramount, but finding a niche for her was quite difficult. Given that the von Sternberg style was no longer profitable, Paramount had to figure out which direction to go with Dietrich.

The films that Dietrich appeared in from 1936 onward all struggle to some extent with this predicament. In 1936, she appeared in three films, the last of which, *The Garden of Allah*, was not made for Paramount but instead for David Selznick, who would become best known a few years later for producing *Gone With the Wind*. But unlike that masterpiece, *The Garden of Allah* was a major flop, which had disastrous consequences on Dietrich's career at the time. That Dietrich was failing to generate profits was not particularly unusual with major stars because it cost a great deal of money to attract the most high-profile stars, requiring the films to do superbly at the box office just to break even. Consequently, Dietrich's career stagnated, and she would not act during 1938.

Selznick

At some point during the late 1930s, possibly as early as 1937, Dietrich was approached by the Nazi Party in order to appear in the films produced by the Third Reich, but she refused to work for the Nazis, who responded by banning her films. As if to further make her point, Dietrich applied for American citizenship in 1937 and received it in 1939, famously stating, "The Germans and I no longer speak the same language." The rise of the Nazi Party alienated Marlene from her sister, who was a committed Nazi, but Marlene would be an ardent supporter of the Allies and even use her own money to help Jewish friends escape the country.

After appearing in no films during 1938, Dietrich made a comeback with the 1939 film *Destry Rides Again*. For the first time, Dietrich was cast in a Western, and while the film was hardly a small production (James Stewart, already a major figure in Hollywood, was her co-star), the production values are not as dazzling as the von Sternberg films. Still, one of the most noteworthy aspects of Dietrich's career is the way in which the vast majority of her films feature her as a cabaret singer with a weak moral compass, or in an analogous role. Accordingly, in *Destry Rides Again*, Marlene plays Frenchie, a dance hall performer who transforms the town into a site of ill repute. Similar to her domestication in the earlier films, Frenchie eventually acquiesces to the law and is tragically killed. Today, the film is remembered for her performance of "See What the Boys in the Back Room Will Have" and "You've Got That Look," both of which were later released on albums. In addition, Dietrich would later confess to having had an affair with James Stewart, although that claim rests on the flimsy testimony of Marlene herself.

Dietrich on the set of *Destry Rides Again*

One of the great ironies of Dietrich's career is that in the immediate aftermath of her comeback, her output was every bit as prolific as it had been in the von Sternberg period, even if it's far more unrecognized. After signing with Universal Studios, she maintained a steady workload, even as she was unable to retain her earlier prominence within the industry. In 1940, she appeared in just one film, but in 1941 she appeared in two, and 1942 saw the release of three of her films. None of the films are often mentioned in discussions of her career, but these years saw her act alongside a variety of famous actors, including John Wayne, Fred MacMurray, George Raft, and Edward G. Robinson. As those names might suggest, during this period Marlene appeared primarily in Westerns, gangster films, and adventure epics. The actors may seem unlikely matches to appear alongside the Prussian glamour of Dietrich, but Marlene did not seem to mind, and it has long been alleged that she and John Wayne were romantically involved. In addition, off the movie set, one of the most significant developments to occur during the 1940s was the wedding of her daughter Maria in 1943. Maria she married a much-older man against Marlene's will. Five years later, Maria gave birth to a child, and Marlene was famously named the "world's most glamorous grandmother."

During World War II, Marlene effusively expressed her support for the Allies. This was necessary considering her German ethnicity, but her advocacy went far beyond empty gestures. In addition to touring for the USO and entertaining soldiers in person in 1944 and 1945, she sold war bonds and appeared in the musical *Follow the Boys* (1944), a collaborative effort made by many luminaries under contract with Universal Studios in order to entertain the troops. Moreover, while touring with the USO, she was unafraid to place herself in the dangerous situation of performing for soldiers on the front lines in Algeria, Britain, France, and Germany. Just as she had worked tirelessly to support the troops during World War I, Marlene was no less active during World War II. Ironically, she even broadcast anti-Nazi speeches for Germany, which had banned her films. After the war, Dietrich received the Medal of Freedom from the United States, and she also received awards from France and Belgium. Discussing Dietrich's life during World War II, one of her grandsons noted, "After all, this is a woman who was born into the post-Bismarck world, and chose between right and wrong at a time when most people around the world didn't - and particularly people in Germany failed. And even though it meant turning her back on her life and family, she knew the difference between right and wrong, and fought for it."

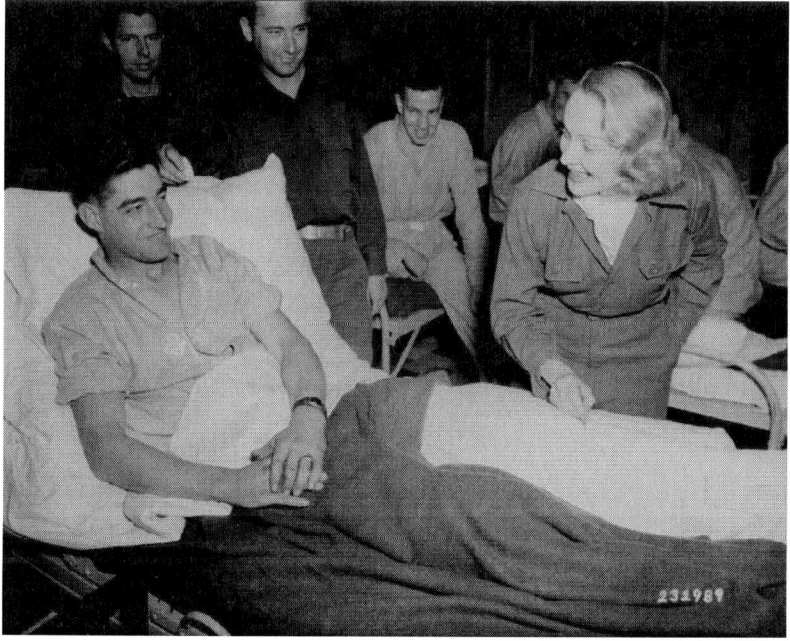

Dietrich visiting soldiers in Belgium, 1944

After World War II, Dietrich appeared in films produced by a number of studios, resulting in a string of films bearing little in common. In 1948, she starred in the topical *A Foreign Affair*, directed by fellow German expatriate Billy Wilder, which featured her as a cabaret singer in postwar Germany who has strong Nazi ties. The film marked a change in Dietrich's star image in that she starred opposite Jean Arthur, who is eventually reunited with the male lead. Not only did this film involve Dietrich losing the male lead to another woman, but the contrast between Jean Arthur and Marlene Dietrich reflected the shifting tastes of the American public. No longer craving the European exoticism of Marlene, a new standard for public taste emerged that privileged clean-cut women such as Doris Day, Jean Arthur, and Jane Wyman.

From the credits of *A Foreign Affair*

Chapter 5: Moving On

"I'm worth more dead than alive. Don't cry for me after I'm gone; cry for me now." – Marlene Dietrich

During the 1950s, Marlene's activity slowed considerably, but she was given the opportunity to work with several of the most famous directors in Hollywood. 1950 saw her appear in Alfred Hitchcock's *Stage Fright*. The film borrowed from *A Foreign Affair* in casting Marlene as an evil woman opposite a "good girl" character, in this case Jane Wyman. Dietrich's more famous films corrected her character flaws, but by not playing the female lead, Marlene began appearing in more one-dimensional roles that highlighted and played upon the aspects of her image that were perceived as ignoble.

In 1952, Marlene appeared in Fritz Lang's *Rancho Notorious*, marking the first time she and the famous German director collaborated. The film not only looks back to the Dietrich-von Sternberg films but also referenced Marlene's post-von Sternberg film *Destry Rides Again*. Not Both films are Westerns, and in each Marlene plays a dance hall singer named Frenchie. Another interesting comparison between *Rancho Notorious* and Marlene's early films is the use of camp. Von Sternberg films were campy in a glamorous manner, while Lang's film feels sloppy in many aspects (particularly the cheap color used), resulting in a somewhat reckless tone.

Dietrich in *Rancho Notorious*

After *Rancho Notorious*, Dietrich went three years without appearing in any films. During this period, she returned to the cabaret stage, where she frequently performed songs that she had sung in her films. After hiring Burt Bacharach as her musical arranger, she began appearing in one-woman shows and released four albums from 1957-1964. Despite having never received any substantial training as a singer, she was extremely successful as a performer, due largely to her elaborate costumes, wigs, and nonsurgical beautifying efforts. Through her costumes, Marlene recreated (albeit in an unpolished manner) the glamour of her early films and by dressing up in this manner, she only strengthened the myth of the younger Marlene. At times, she was being paid $30,000 a week for her performances, which she took on the road to several different countries.

By forever masking herself in costume, she never let audiences see the "real" Marlene, and in so doing, she retained the air of mystery that surrounds her to this day. In addition, by embracing her campy image, Dietrich evolved into a major icon within the gay and lesbian community. Her lesbian popularity was also impacted by the 1955 revelation that Dietrich had engaged in lesbian relationships throughout her life, a belated discovery but one that was significant nonetheless. Considering the professional risk associated with being "outed" during the 1950s, however, revealing that Dietrich was bisexual constituted an implicit admission that she was no longer a major Hollywood actress (Weiss).

Marlene's next movie was *Witness for the Prosecution* (1956), which reunited her with Billy Wilder and cast her in the role of a jealous wife who commits a crime of passion. The film was a major commercial and critical success and was nominated for several Academy Awards, though Dietrich was not nominated for her performance. Her final two films before unofficially retiring (aside from a cameo in *Paris When it Sizzles* (1964)) were *Touch of Evil* (1958) and *Judgment at Nuremberg* (1961). In both films, she appears alongside a large ensemble cast, with her presence serving more as a reminder of her past fame rather than a major component of her body of work. Her performance in *Touch of Evil* is the better-known of the two, as she delivers the memorable closing line "He was some kind of man." While these final films were relatively well-regarded, by 1960 Marlene was already nearing the age of 60. Her film career was effectively over.

Dietrich in *Touch of Evil*

With her film career all but over, Marlene ventured into both German and American television during the 1960s and early 1970s. She also acted in theater and was honored with a special Tony Award in 1968. But she began suffering significant health problems by the 1960s, particularly her diagnosis of cervical cancer in 1965. She became increasingly dependent on alcohol and painkillers, and during one performance in 1973 she actually fell of the stage. Her final stage appearance came in September of 1975, when she fell off the stage while performing in Sydney. Her husband died the following year, but they had been estranged for decades.

Dietrich in 1960

The late 1970s saw Dietrich make a brief return to the cinema when she played a small part in the 1978 film *Just a Gigolo*, starring David Bowie. By this time, however, she became increasingly reclusive and would famously never leave her residence. She would conduct phone conversations for hours on end but never venture outside her 4 room apartment in Paris. Meals were cooked on a hot plate next to her bed, and by remaining reclusive, Dietrich managed to strengthen the secrecy that surrounded her name. Late in life, she was relatively poor, due to decades of free spending, but she also kept her expenses minimal by remaining in her apartment. minimal. As she had once so aptly put it, "There is a gigantic difference between earning a great deal of money and being rich."

In 1984, Dietrich lent her voice to a documentary about her titled *Marlene*, but she refused to actually appear in the documentary. Dietrich had long been outspoken about religion, or her lack of interest in it, at one point asserting, "If there is a supreme being, he's crazy." She was also an ardent supporter of astrology and even went so far as to let friends know their horoscopes, one time claiming, "After all, everyone knows that the moon pulls the sea away from the land, and farmers don't plant when the moon is wrong. Why should humans escape?" However, in her final years, Dietrich converted to Catholicism and became quite religious. Despite living with persistent health problems, Marlene reached her 90s, eventually dying in 1992 of renal failure.

It is telling that in the years before and after Marlene Dietrich's career, there has never been an actress remotely like her. Her icy countenance and the glowing way in which von Sternberg filmed her made her almost impossibly glamorous. Over the course of her long and circuitous career, she underwent many ups and downs, yet she managed to maintain an impenetrable quality to her image. Moreover, few have been so relentless in building their myth. More than two decades after her death, there are still numerous aspects of her life that remain murky. Always self-conscious in cultivating her image, one gets the sense that Marlene delighted in deliberatively confusing the public about her personal life and back story. When one of her grandsons was asked if there was another side to Dietrich that the public never saw, he explained:

> "I think the only people who understood her fully were her peers. And her peers may have been Howard Arlen, Noel Coward or Burt Bacharach. Or in the case of actors, John Wayne, Clark Gable and Jimmy Stewart and so on. People recognised in her the same abilities they also had, but most of them stood in awe of her multi-discipline abilities. She was one of those rare persons who was able to excel at more than one art form, simultaneously. When you hear people like Kenneth Tynan talk about her, they talk about her as a woman. She wasn't simply an actress, a monster, a celebrity…I think Katharine Hepburn understood Marlene better than most people because she recognised in her that true woman of the year ability…She was never aloof. She never ever had any corrective surgery, but one morning she realised she could no longer maintain the visual persona of Marlene Dietrich. So she simply remodelled the visual persona from the public eye, that's all. She did answer 100 letters a day and spent thousands of dollars on telephone calls, so she certainly wasn't a recluse."

Examining Marlene Dietrich's life in conjunction with her films is illuminating in a number of ways and helps clarify certain aspects of her life and personality. For one, it is certain that her beauty was inherited from her father, while she received her work ethic from her mother. In addition, while she was emotionless on screen, she was effusive in expressing her affection for adult figures growing up, including her grandmother and schoolteacher. Marlene may have been one of the most famous femme fatales of all time, but she was clearly capable of expressing emotion, even if she never displayed much of it in her films, and for all the exoticism of her film career, late in life Marlene lived a distinctly banal existence, never leaving her room and cooking her meals herself in her apartment.

While the many biographies released in recent decades all shed light on some aspects of Marlene Dietrich's life, and many of them reveal very ordinary things, her life is ultimately defined by its ambiguity. Was she happy in life or depressed? Did her sexual orientation skew more heavily toward being gay or straight? The obsessive control she exerted over her personal life makes it impossible to truly answer these questions, and there is a similar mystique that surfaces between her films and personal life. In the impulsive rush to arrive at a definitive answer to the unresolved questions surrounding her life, it is perhaps difficult to accept that so much of Marlene's life remains impossible to conclusively determine. At the same time, the ambiguity of Dietrich's life is strangely fitting; it is, after all, appropriate that no matter how hard one tries to unlock the secrets of her life, the myth of Marlene remains alive and well.

Bibliography

Bach, Steven. *Marlene Dietrich: Life and Legend.* Minneapolis: University of Minnesota Press, 1992. Print.

Bell-Metereau, Rebecca. *Hollywood Androgyny.* New York: Columbia University Press, 1985. Print.

Chandler, Charlotte. *Marlene: Marlene Dietrich, A Personal Biography.* New York: Simon & Schuster, 2011. Print.

Dietrich, Marlene. *Marlene.* New York: Open Road Media, 2012. Web.

Kuzniar, Alice A. *The Queer German Cinema.* Stanford: Stanford University Press, 2000. Print.

Mulvey, Laura. *Visual and Other Pleasures.* Bloomington: Indiana University Press, 1989. Print.

Naremore, Jarmes. *Acting in the Cinema.* Berkeley: University of California Press, 1990. Print.

Riva, J. David, and Guy Stern, eds. *A Woman at War: Marlene Dietrich Remembered.* Detroit: Wayne State University Press, 2006. Print.

Ryan, David Stuart. *The Blue Angel: The Life and Films of Marlene Dietrich.* London: Kozmik Press, 2010. Web.

Skaerved, Malene Sheppard. *Dietrich.* London: Haus Publishing Limited, 2003. Print.

Sontag, Susan. *Against Interpretation and Other Essays.* New York: Picador Press, 2001. Print.

Weiss, Andrea. "A Queer Feeling When I Look at You: Hollywood Stars and the Lesbian Spectatorship of the 1930s." *Stardom: Industry of Desire.* Ed. Christine Gledhill. London: Routledge, 1991. Print.

Made in United States
North Haven, CT
11 July 2022